T0106303

OF TRUTH AND RIGHTEOUSNESS

JOSEPH L. REAVES SR.

WestBow
PRESS
A DIVISION OF THOMAS NELSON

Copyright © 2012 by Joseph L. Reaves Sr..

All rights reserved. No part of this book may be used or reproduced by any means, graphic, electronic, or mechanical, including photocopying, recording, taping or by any information storage retrieval system without the written permission of the publisher except in the case of brief quotations embodied in critical articles and reviews.

WestBow Press books may be ordered through booksellers or by contacting:

WestBow Press
A Division of Thomas Nelson
1663 Liberty Drive
Bloomington, IN 47403
www.westbowpress.com
1-(866) 928-1240

Because of the dynamic nature of the Internet, any web addresses or links contained in this book may have changed since publication and may no longer be valid. The views expressed in this work are solely those of the author and do not necessarily reflect the views of the publisher, and the publisher hereby disclaims any responsibility for them.

Any people depicted in stock imagery provided by Thinkstock are models, and such images are being used for illustrative purposes only.

Certain stock imagery © Thinkstock.

ISBN: 978-1-4497-2946-2 (sc)
ISBN: 978-1-4497-2947-9 (hc)
ISBN: 978-1-4497-2945-5 (e)

Library of Congress Control Number: 2011918906

Printed in the United States of America

WestBow Press rev. date:3/19/2012

OF TRUTH AND RIGHTEOUSNESS

INSPIRED BY THE BLESSED HOLY SPIRIT

Howbeit when He the Spirit of truth, is come, He will guide you into all truth: for He shall not speak of Himself, but whatsoever He shall hear, that shall He speak: and He will show you things to come.

John 16:13.

This book and its writing is to acknowledge the divine call and work of those dedicated men and women in the power of the HOLY SPIRIT to carry the word of GOD, the gospel of our Blessed Savior and LORD JESUS CHRIST to all nations.

Acts 1:6-8.

INTRODUCTION

These writing for this book is taken from the King James Version of the Bible. Moses wrote the first five books of the bible, as GOD Almighty gave him the authority to record all the pertinent truth that would come forth out of the mouth of GOD. We should see from the beginning of Moses experience with the call on his life to serve the GOD of Israel, as a deliverer for the children of Jacob out of Egyptian bondage. In the book of Exodus there is records of the family and parents of Aaron, Miriam, and Moses. As Moses grew up in the house of Pharaoh with his adopted mother, the daughter of Pharaoh, he begun to notice the harsh treatment of the Hebrew people in Egypt under the power of the Egyptian taskmaster. Moses had a burden in his heart, because Moses had found out he was a Hebrew alone with thousands of other Hebrews. Moses knew he was free as the son of the daughter of Pharaoh, however, this is not freedom at all for Moses nor the children of Israel because of the false gods of Egypt, that was worshiped everyday for what ever reason. These children of Jacob was in physical bondage, and spiritual bondage at the same time; there in Egypt, because they were not worshiping the LORD GOD of Israel.

Moses the son of Pharaoh daughter saw an Egyptians assaulting a Hebrew slave; this act of violence was unexceptable with Moses, so he killed the Egyptians soldier, and hid his body in the sand, as if no one saw it. The next day there were two Hebrew men fighting each other when

Moses saw them fighting he ask why are you fighting your brethren? One of the Hebrew men said loudly to Moses will you kill me as you killed the Egyptian soldier yesterday.

Moses knew this news of him killing an Egyptian soldier would get to the ears of Pharaoh, King of Egypt; so Moses fled for his life out into the desert, so he would not be found by Pharaoh.

Moses found himself near a well of water that was covered up. This is the well of water where all the herdsmen and herdswomen came to water their herds. The daughters of Jethro, the priest of Midian also came to water their herds. Jethro gave his daughter Zipporah to be Moses wife,and she bare him two sons.

Moses was there in Egypt for the first forty years of his life. Now we see the second forty years of Moses life on the backside of the mountain. During this backside of the mountain experience here is where GOD cause a fire in a bush that Moses saw, and the fire did not consume the bush.

Moses said I must get closer to see this great sight; because the bush is on fire from morning until evening and is not consumed. As Moses approach the burning bush the GOD of Israel called to him, and told him to remove your shoes from off your feet because you are on Holy ground.

GOD told Moses He wanted him to return to Egypt to free the children of Israel from the house of bondage. Moses made all sorts of excuses for not to be the right person for the task ahead. If anyone who would or could know your capabilities is GOD Himself.

GOD has a plan for His people Israel for the sake of promise that He had made to Abraham, Isaac, and Jacob; that GOD would make a nation in Egypt; in the midst of stranger and bring them out to a land flowing with milk and honey. The GOD of the Hebrews told Moses to call his brother Aaron to go with him. Aaron would serve as a priest to Moses; while Moses would serve as a God to Pharaoh.

Then GOD prepare His servants Moses and Aaron to go to Pharaoh King of Egypt and tell him to let My people go that they may come and worship Me.

First of all GOD Himself tells Moses, for the first time, "I AM THE LORD."

Exodus 6:2.

No one ever in the history of Holy Bible has ever been told those words only Moses.

Second of all GOD said in Exodus 6:3-And I appeared unto Abraham, unto Isaac, and unto Jacob, by the name of GOD Almighty, but by My name LORD was I not known to them.

In Genesis 1:26; Moses wrote about Us: this Us that Moses is addressing is none other than the Godhead, which consist of GOD the Father which is Elohim, GOD the Son which is CHRIST JESUS our LORD and Savior, and GOD the HOLY SPIRIT which is the Spirit of Truth, our Helper.

This book of Truth and Righteousness is given by the Holy Spirit, to whoever will receive this revelation of truth. Because the Spirit of GOD is saying that none of the Godhead is known by the name Jehovah ; past, present, or future.

SECTION ONE

GOD The Father-(ELOHIM)

In this section of reading you will notice the work of GOD in creating all things by His word.

In the beginning GOD created the heaven and the earth.

Genesis 1:1

And GOD spoke and all His creation was manifest and He saw that it was good.

Genesis 1:3-25.

And GOD said, Let Us make man in Our image, after Our likeness: and let them have dominion over the fish of the sea, and over the fowl of the air, and over the cattle, and over all the earth, and over every creeping thing that creepeth upon the earth.

Genesis 1:26.

So GOD created man in His own image, in the image of GOD created He him; male and female created He them.

Genesis 1:27.

The very first thing that GOD does for His first family, the Adams family is to bless them with His divine favor, and then He said take authority over all creation. Genesis 1:28-31, and GOD (Elohim) finished all His work, and rested, sanctifying the seventh day for rest and worship.

Genesis 2:1-3.

When we look at the generations of the heavens and of the earth when they were created, in the day that the LORD GOD (CHRIST JESUS) made the earth and the heavens,

Genesis 2:4-14: John 1:3.

Now the LORD GOD (CHRIST JESUS) commanded the man, saying, of every tree of the garden thou mayest freely eat;

But of the tree of the knowledge of good and evil, thou shalt not eat of it: for in the day that thou eatest thereof thou shalt surely die.

Genesis 2:16-17.

And the LORD GOD (CHRIST JESUS) said, It is not good that the man should be alone; I will make him an help meet for him.

Genesis 2:18.

Now Adam named every living creature, and that was the name thereof. Genesis 2:19-20, in Genesis 2:21-25, the LORD GOD (CHRIST JESUS) perform the very first surgery in the garden of Eden, by removing a rib from the man Adam, that He might bring forth a woman to be a wife to Adam the man.

And the serpent lend his body to Satan, that he might deceive Eve (the mother of us all) and cause her to doubt the word of the LORD GOD (CHRIST JESUS), because Eve called to her husband and he did eat of the tree of knowledge of good and evil, because Satan said that the LORD GOD did not want them to be wise, knowing good and evil, becoming as gods, Ye shall not surely die.

Genesis 3:1-7.

SECTION TWO THRU THREE C

GOD The SON-LORD GOD-SAVIOR

This second section present the Savior of the world, given to us by GOD the Father to die for all sinners. But with the precious blood of Christ, as of a lamb without blemish and wihtout spot:

Who verily was foreordained before the foundation of the world, but was manifest in these last times for you.

Who by Him do believe in GOD, that raised Him up from the dead, and gave Him glory; that your faith and hope might be in GOD.

If Eve (the mother of us all) had listen to the LORD GOD (CHRIST JESUS) when the LORD GOD said you shall not eat of the tree of knowledge of good and evil. Eve told satan that they were told not to eat of the tree in the midst of the garden, and they were not to touch it.

In Genesis 2:9, and out of the ground made the LORD GOD (CHRIST JESUS) to grow every tree that is pleasant to the sight, and good for food; the tree of life also in the midst of the garden, and the tree of knowledge of good and evil.

Beloved, the tree of life also in the midst of the garden, the tree of life, not the tree of death. Beloved, Genesis 2:9, Mother Eve lied about the tree of life.

Who His own self bare our sins in His own body on the tree, that we, being dead to sins, should live unto righteousness: by whose stripes ye were healed.

I Peter 2:24.

And after the fall of Adam, which means Adam had disobeyed the LORD GOD (CHRIST JESUS) and sinned against GOD (ELOHIM). Adam the representative of all made in the image and likeness of the triune GOD.

And the very GOD of peace sanctify you wholly; and I pray GOD your whole spirit and soul and body be preserved blameless unto the coming of our LORD JESUS CHRIST.

I Thessalonians 5:23.

And the LORD GOD (CHRIST JESUS) promised Adam and Eve that He would be their Savior and Kinsman Redeemer.

Genesis 3:15-22.

And I, if I be lifted up from the earth, will draw all men unto Me.

John 12:32.

This is a covenant of grace and mercy from the LORD GOD of Israel to all His creature for all times, which is found here in the book of Exodus 34:5-7.

And the LORD descended in the cloud and stood with him there, and proclaimed the name of the LORD.

And the LORD passed by before him and proclaimed, the LORD, the LORD GOD, merciful and gracious, long suffering, and abundant in goodness and truth.

Keeping mercy for thousands, forgiving iniquity and transgression and sin, and that will by no means clear the guilty; visiting the iniquity of the fathers upon the children, and upon the children's children, unto the third and to the fourth generation.

SECTION THREE D THRU FIVE

GOD The HOLY SPIRIT-SPIRIT of Truth our Helper

Here in this third section of reading we see the Spirit of GOD active in creation, and indwelling the believer. And I will pray the Father, and He shall give you another Comforter, that He may abide with you foever;

Even the Spirit of truth; whom the world cannot receive, because it seeth Him not, neither knoweth Him: but ye know Him; for He dwelleth with you, and shall be in you.

Fear and anguish grip the heart and the finite mind of Moses the LORD'S servant as he felt the awesome present of HOLY GOD. As Moses humble himself before the LORD, he make a covenant request for Israel and for himself.

And Moses made haste, and bowed his head toward the earth, and worshiped.

And he said, If now I have found grace in Thy sight, O LORD, let my LORD, I pray Thee, go among us; for it is a stiffnecked people; and pardon our iniquity and our sin, and take us for thine inheritance.

And He said, Behold, I make a covenant: before all thy people, I will do marvels, such as have not been done in all the earth, nor in any nation: and all the people among which thou art shall see the work of the LORD: for it is a terrible thing that I will do with thee.

Exodus 34:8-10.

When the Lord made this covenant with Moses and with the children of Israel He made it clear that the covenant of blessing were sure and permanent, however, if Israel made a covenant with nations, they would bring a curse upon Israel, because other nations did not know the LORD GOD of Israel, the only Living and True GOD.

I Thessalonians 1:9.

And the Lord said unto Moses, Write thou these words: for after the tenor of these words I have made a covenant with thee and with Israel.

And he was there with the LORD forty days and forty nights; he did neither eat bread, nor drink water. And he wrote upon the tables the words of the covenant, the ten commandments.

Exodus 34:11-28.

And thou shalt say unto Pharaoh, Thus saith the LORD, of Israel is My son, even My firstborn:

Exodus 4:22.

Our Savior and LORD JESUS CHRIST tells us how the HOLY SPIRIT, the Spirit of truth our Helper will come from the Father in the name of the LORD to work intricately in the hearts and minds of those saints, past, present, and future.

When we look in Holy Scripture we note how the Holy Spirit is at work, first in creation.

And the earth was without form, and void; and darkness was upon the face of the deep.

And the Spirit of GOD moved upon the face of the waters.

Genesis 1:2.

Who laid the foundations of the earth, that it should not be removed for ever.

Thou covereth it with the deep as with a garment: the waters stood above the mountains.

At Thy rebuke they fled; at the voice of Thy thunder they hasted away.

They go up by the mountains; they go down by the valley unto the place which Thou hast founded for them.

Thou hast set a bound that they may not pass over; that they turn not again to cover the earth.

Psalm 104:5-9.

Now Moses is told by the LORD of a man named Bezaleel the son of Uri of the tribe of Judah:

And I have filled him with the Spirit of GOD, in wisdom, and in understanding, and in knowledge, and in all manner of workmsnship.

Joseph the son of Jacob was blessed by the LORD GOD of Israel with the Spirit.

And Pharaoh said unto his servants, can we find such a one as this is, a man in whom the Spirit of GOD is?

David, the king of Israel the servant of the LORD, found himself one who had sinned before the Holy present of the LORD, when he had taken the wife of Uriah, Bathsheba to his bed and she was with child.

2nd Samuel 11:3-5.

David repented, Hide Thy face from my sins, and blot out all mine iniquities. Create in me a clean heart, O GOD: and renew a right spirit within me.

Cast me not away from Thy presence; and take not Thy Holy Spirit from me.

Psalm 51:9-11.

When the children of Israel became rebellious against the goodness of the LORD, we see how the LORD respond to their disobedience.

But they rebelled, and vexed His Holy Spirit: therefore He was turned to be their enemy, and He fought against them.

Isaiah 63:10.

And the people murmured against Moses saying, What shall we drink?

Exodus 15:24.

In the ministry of the LORD JESUS CHRIST our all times example of how to follow the guidance and leadership of the blessed Holy Spirit.

How GOD anointed JESUS of Nazareth with the Holy Ghost and with power: who went about doing good, and healing all that were oppressed of the devil; for GOD was with Him.

Acts 10:38.

Beloved, We know that the Holy Spirit came on the day of Pentecost to indwell all the church of JESUS CHRIST.

And they were all filled with the Holy Ghost, and began to speak with other tongues, as the Spirit gave them utterance.

Acts 2:4.

Beloved, Let us be sure that our utterance is of the Holy Spirit, and not our imagination nor our feeling because both can lie and deceive those we think we are trying to show the love of GOD.

I John 3:18.

And if thou say in thine heart, How shall we know the word which the LORD hath not spoken?

When a prophet speaketh in the name of the LORD, if the thing follow not, nor come to pass, that is the thing which the LORD hath not spoken, but the prophet hath spoken it presumptuously: thou shalt not be afraid of him.

Deuteronomy 18:17-22.

I AM THE LORD!

And Abram was called by the LORD out of Haran, to a land that the LORD would show him.

Now the LORD had said unto Abram, Get thee out of thy country, and from thy kindred, and from thy fathers house, unto a land that I will show thee:

And I will make of thee a great nation, and I will bless thee, and make thy name great; and thou shalt be a blessing:

And I will bless them that bless thee, and curse him that curseth thee: and in thee shall all families of the earth be blessed.

Genesis 12:1-3.

Abram, before he is named Abraham, Abram showed great faith, because he walks by faith and not by sight, for he follows the very word and voice of the LORD.

There was a time in Abram life that he did not put his trust in GOD.

And there was a famine in the land: and Abram went down into Egypt to sojourn there: for the famine was grievous in the land.

Genesis 12:10.

SECTION SIX THRU EIGHT

Here Almighty GOD make a covenant with Abram, coupled with exceeding great and precious promises for all the Hebrew children, and non—Hebrew families.

It is said that Abram concocted a lie with his wife Sarai, because Sarai was a beautiful woman, so Abram feared he would be killed because of her beauty.

However, Abram told the truth about himself and Sarai his sister. The truth is Sarai is 100% Abram sister, and Sarai is 100% Abram wife.

Genesis 12:12-20.

Abram did not lie as some had said in the interpretation of GOD'S word concerning Abram.

And Abram was very rich in cattle, in silver, and in gold.

Genesis 13:2.

And Abram worship the LORD for all His goodness for him and Sarai his wife.

Genesis 13:3-4.

When the LORD promised to bless Abram, Lot was also bless because of the association with Abram.

Genesis 13:5-6.

Abram and Lot separated because of the quarreling of their herdsmen.

Lot, look to Sodom and Gomorrah, before the LORD destroyed it. Lot, chose the plain of Jordan and journeyed east.

Genesis 13:7-11.

While Lot, the nephew of Abram journeyed east, the LORD said to Abram look for all the land you see I will give thee and thy descendants.

Genesis 13:14-18.

It has been said that one has not heard any news from near Kin all things are good.

This is not for Lot and his family, now living in Sodom and Gomorrah. There were four Kings against five Kings of Sodom and Gomorrah and they took Lot, and all that he had.

Genesis 14:1-11.

And one of the person that had escaped Sodom came and told Abram about the invading of the enemies.

Genesis 14:12

Abram was a man of preparedness. He had 318 young men trained for war. Abram had allies that fought with him for the very same causes.

Genesis 14:13-17.

Abram is victorious in the war against the enemy of Lot his nephew, and for all the families of Sodom and Gomorrah, because all the kings and their soldier fled from the heat of the battle in their cowardness, however, Abram had GOD on his side, to give him the victory.

Genesis 14:18-20.

Here we see CHRIST Himself, the Melchizedek of the Old Testament, King of Salem (Jerusalem).

Genesis 14:18.

For this Melchizedek, King of Salem, priest of the Most High GOD, who met Abraham returning from the slaughter of the Kings, and blessed him;

To whom also Abraham gave a tenth part of all: first being by interpretation King of Righteousness, and after that also King of Salem, which is King of Peace:

Without father, without mother, without descendants, having neither beginning of days, nor end of life; but made like unto the Son of GOD; abideth a priest continually.

Hebrews 7:1-3.

Beloved, when the world speak favorable to you and try to give to you that which they do not have, refuse to receive it because it will only separate you from GOD Almighty and His blessed hope for your life.

Genesis 14:21-24.

After these things the word of the LORD came unto Abram in a vision, saying, Fear not, Abram: I am thy shield, and thy exceeding great reward.

Genesis 15:1.

Abram ask the LORD GOD for children even through his servant Eliezer.

Genesis 15:2-3.

And the LORD answered Abram with faithful news of himself and his wife Sarai becoming parents.

Genesis 15:4.

When Abram saw the vision of heaven, its stars, that he could not number, these are the descendants of yours.

Genesis 15:5.

And he believed in the LORD; and He counted it to him for righteousness.

Genesis 15:6.

And He said unto him, I AM THE LORD that brought thee out of Ur of the Chaldees, to give thee this land to inherit it.

Genesis 15:7.

And he said, LORD GOD, whereby shall I know that I shall inherit it?

Genesis 15:8.

And He said unto him, Take Me an heifer of three years old, and a she goat of three years old, and a ram of three years old, and a turtledove, and a young pigeon.

Genesis 15:9.

And he took unto him all these, and divided them in the midst, and laid each piece one against another: but the birds divided he not.

Genesis 15:10.

The LORD GOD (CHRIST JESUS), establish His covenant with Abram in blood of these animals and later in the Son of GOD.

John 3:16.

These animals also represent the kind of blood sacrifices that the children of Israel are to offer for burnt offering and sin offering whether the person of Israel were rich or poor.

The ram is CHRIST, in the since that the ram was in the midst of the animal which was on each side of the ram.

Genesis 15:9-10.

Behold the Lamb of GOD, which taketh away the sin of the world.

John 1:29.

And when the fowls came down upon the carcases, Abram drove them away.

Genesis 15:11.

Abram uses his authority in driving out those demon spirit from interrupting the covenant blessing that await him.

And when he sowed, some seeds fell by the way side, and the fowls came and devoured them up:

Matthew 13:4.

Abram is told by the LORD that he would not see all of his descendants, but he would see his seed. They would be in a strange land in the midst of strange people, but the LORD would bring to the land of promise with great possessions. Abram would sleep with his fathers in peace at an old age.

But in the fourth generation they shall come hither again: for the iniquity of the Amorites is not yet full.

Genesis 15:12-16.

And it came to pass, that when the sun went down, and it was dark, behold a smoking furnace, and a burning lamp that passed between those pieces.

Genesis 15:17.

The LORD GOD sealed the blood covenant with His glorious present as He passed between those pieces that He had ordained to be exceptable in His Holy sight.

Genesis 15:18.

In the same day the LORD made a covenant with Abram, saying, Unto thy seed have I given this land, from the river of Egypt unto the great river, the river Euphrates:

Genesis 15:18-21.

I AM THE LORD!

Let us begin with the life of Moses, born in Egypt, born in slavery, born to be one of the most faithful servants of Almighty GOD.

SECTION NINE THRU THIRTEEN

In this fifth section of reading we come to the death of Joseph, all his brethren, and all that generation. We will also see the parents of Moses, his birth, and his fleeing from Pharaoh to the desert, where he takes a wife, and return to Egypt for the children of GOD, to bring them out of bondage for the worship of the GOD of the Hebrew.

I AM THE LORD!

Now there arose up a new King over Egypt, which knew not Joseph.

Exodus 1:8.

And Joseph died, and all his brethren, and all that generation . . .

Exodus 1:6.

This new King of Egypt did not know Joseph during his life as the governor of Egypt, so the favor that Israel had with the pass Pharaoh was lost, however help is on its way.

And he said, When ye do the office of a midwife to the Hebrew women, and see them upon the stools; if it be a son, then ye shall kill him: but if it be a daughter, then she shall live. Exodus 10:16-16.

But the midwives feared GOD, (Elohim) and did not as the King of Egypt commanded them, but saved the men children alive.

Exodus 1:17.

And there went a man of the house of Levi, and took to wife a daughter of the Levi.

And the woman conceived, and bare a son: and when she saw him that he was a goodly child, she hid him three months. Exodus 2:12.

And Am'ram took him Joch'e-bed his father's sister to wife; and she bare him Aaron and Moses: and the years of the life of Am'ram were and hundred and thirty and seven years.

Exodus 6:20.

Joch'e-bed put her son in an ark of reeds, sent him down the nile river, his sister Miriam watched over him to see what would happen to her brother, Pharaoh's daughter came to the river for a bath, her and her maids, she saw the ark, sent one of her maids to bring the ark to her, that she might see inside, there she saw a Hebrew son that delighted her heart and she loved him and kept him, knowing the child had needs she could not provide, the sister offered to get the child mother that she might nurse the boy, and she was willing to pay the mother for her motherly services, she Joch'e-bed return her son to the Pharaoh daughter, and she named him Moses, because she drew him out of the water.

Exodus 2:3-10.

And it came to pass in those days, when Moses was grown, that he went out unto his brethren, and looked on their burdens: and he spied an Egyptian, smiting an Hebrew, one of his brethren.

And he looked this way and that way, and when he saw that there was no man, he slew the Egyptian, and hid him in the sand.

Exodus 2:11-12.

When Moses did the unthinkable by killing an Egyptian that was beating a Hebrew man, his thoughts were to help his fellow country man. The same Hebrew man fighting with another Hebrew man became angry with Moses as he stop the fight. The man told on Moses, Moses feared for his life, because Pharaoh had heard and wanted Moses killed, however Moses had fled for his life.

Exodus 2:13-15.

Now Moses landed in Midian and he sat down by a well where all the herdsmen came to water their live stock. There is a priest in Midain with seven daughters no sons, and these daughters waters their father's flock every day at this well.

And the shepherds came and drove them away: but Moses stood up and helped them, and watered their flock.

Exodus 2:16-19.

Moses was called to the home of the priest for the kindness that he had shown to his daughters.

Exodus 2L21-22.

And it came to pass in process of time, that the King of Egypt died: and the children of Israel sighed by reason of the bondage, and they cried, and their cry came up unto GOD by reason of the bondage.

Exodus 2:23.

Because of the covenant that Almighty GOD had made with Abram. Genesis 15:18; and GOD heard their groaning, and GOD remembered His covenant with Abraham, with Isaac and with Jacob.

Exodus 2:24-25.

And GOD looked upon the children of Israel, and GOD had respect unto them.

Exodus 2:25.

Moses had spent the first forty years of his life in Egypt where he was born into slavery, but the GOD of the Hebrews had a better plan for Moses even in the midst of his slave master. Because the LORD had Moses slave master's daughter to be his mother.

Now we notice the second forty years of Moses life, Moses is now a shepherd watching over his father-in-law flock. The LORD GOD of Israel is training Moses to be the pastor for the children of Israel.

Exodus 3:1.

And the angel of the LORD appeared unto him in a flame of fire out of the midst of a bush; and he looked, and behold, the bush burned with fire, and the bush was not consumed.

Exodus 3:2.

And Moses said, I will now turn aside, and see this great sight, why the bush is not burnt.

Exodus 3:3.

And when the LORD saw that he turned aside to see, GOD called unto him out of the midst of the bush, and said, Moses, Moses, and he said, Here am I.

And He said, Draw not near hither: put off thy shoes from off thy feet, for the place where on thy standest is Holy ground.

Exodus 3:4-5.

Be silent, O all flesh, before the LORD: for He is raised up out of His Holy habitation.

Zechariah 2:13.

This is the first of many appearance that the LORD will do in the present of Moses His chosen servant to be a deliverer for the children of Israel out of the house of bondage which is Egypt. And GOD commissions Moses to go to Egypt to let My people go.

Exodus 3:6.

Now after Moses begin to doubt himself the LORD encourage Moses to have faith in GOD.

Mark 11:22.

And Moses said unto GOD, Who am I, that I should go unto Pharaoh, and that I should bring forth the children of Israel out of Egypt?

Exodus 3:11.

And He said, Certainly I will be with thee; and this shall be a token unto thee; that I have sent thee: When thou hast brought forth the people out of Egypt, ye shall serve GOD upon this mountain.

Exodus 3:12.

And Moses want to know what will I say to Israel when they ask who sent you to us? And GOD said unto Moses, I Am That I Am: and He said, Thus shalt thou say unto the children of Israel, I Am hath sent me unto you.

Exodus 3:13-14.

And GOD said moreover unto Moses thus shalt thou say unto the children of Israel, The LORD GOD of your fathers, the GOD of Abraham, the GOD of Isaac, and the GOD of Jacob, hath sent me unto you: this is My name for ever, and this is My memorial unto all generations.

Exodus 3:15.

Moses is told by the LORD GOD of your fathers, the GOD of Abraham, of Isaac, and of Jacob, Go to the elders of Israel and tell them that I the LORD have come to bring you up of the affliction of Egypt, to a land of covenant promise, a land flowing with milk and honey, a land of wealth and riches.

Exodus 3:16-18.

When you, Moses go before the King of Egypt and tell him that the LORD GOD of the Hebrews said, Let My people go.

And I am sure that the King of Egypt will not let you go, no, not by a mighty hand.

Exodus 3:19

The covenant that Almighty GOD made with Abraham is repeated here to Moses of the contents of the covenant.

And I will give this people favor in the sight of the Egyptian: and it shall come to pass, that when ye go, ye shall not go empty: Now faith is the substance of things hoped for, the evidence of things

But every women shall borrow of her neighbor, and of her that sojourneth in her house jewels of silver, and jewels of gold, and raiment: and ye shall put them upon your sons and daughters; and ye shall spoil the Egyptians.

Exodus 3:20-22.

When a man of GOD begin to believe his unbelief, Satan begin to jump up and down in jubilate rejoicing, because Moses faith is some what undeveloped in the GOD who has already shown him how awesome He is. First, Moses sees the bush on fire that is not consumed by the fire, Second, Moses sees the shepherd's rod in his hand turned into a serpent, and, Third, Moses sees his hand become leprous, as white as snow, and turned back to its normal flesh. Then this Moses said to the LORD he could not speak eloquently to Pharaoh King of Egypt, that the King would not let the children of Israel go.

Exodus 4:1-11.

Now therefore go, and I will be with thy mouth, and teach thee what thou shalt say.

Exodus 4:12.

Moses ask the LORD to send someone else.

Exodus 4:13.

And the anger of the LORD was kindled against Moses, and He said, Is not Aaron the Levite thy brother? I know that he can speak well. And also, behold, he cometh forth to meet thee: and when he seeth thee, he will be glad in his heart.

The LORD said to Moses tell Aaron the plan, and put words in his mouth: I will be with your mouth and his mouth to teach you what to do.

And he shall be thy spokesman unto the people: and he shall be, even shall be to thee instead of a mouth, and thou shalt be to him instead of GOD.

And thou shalt take this rod in thine hand, wherewith thou shalt do signs.

Exodus 4:15-17.

Moses return to Jethro his father-in-law and ask him to let him return to Egypt.

The LORD said to Moses leave, go to Egypt, because all the men are dead who sought to kill you. Moses take his wife and his sons and all his possession to return to Egypt to tell Pharaoh King of Egypt to let go the people of the LORD. The first born of the LORD, that they might worship Him.

Isaiah 43:15.

And while Moses and his family was in the Way, the LORD met him to kill him, because he had not circumcised his sons. Exodus 4:18-26.

Now we recall when the LORD told Moses to put words in Aaron mouth.

Exodus 4:15a.

Here n Exodus 4:27-31; And Moses told Aaron all the words of the LORD, who had sent him with all the signs that the LORD commanded him.

Verse 28.

And the people believe, and heard the word of the LORD, and worshiped Him.

Verse 31.

Now Moses and Aaron is ready to face Pharaoh, King of Egypt with conquering words of faith.

Hebrews 11:1.

And afterward Moses and Aaron went in, and told Pharaoh, Thus said the LORD GOD of Israel, Let My people go, that they may hold a feast unto Me in the wilderness.

And Pharaoh said, Who is the LORD, that I should obey His voice to let Israel go? I know not the LORD, neither will I let Israel go.

And they said, The GOD of the Hebrews hath met with us: let us go, we pray thee, three days journey into the desert, and sacrifice unto the LORD our GOD; lest He fall upon us with pestilence, or with the sword.

Exodus 5:1-3.

Then Pharaoh called for the Egyptian taskmasters to make the burdens of labor be multiplied upon the backs of the children of Israel, because of his resentment of the request by the GOD of the Hebrews. Four hundred years of free labor any nations of people would hold on to the workers as long as possible, not knowing that the children of Israel had a GOD which is much more awesome than any of the pretend gods of Egypt or any other nation of people, who hold to their gods like the Egyptians.

Exodus 5:4-19.

When our emotion take over our faith we will overreact, because Moses goes before the LORD and tells the LORD how evil Pharaoh has become since the LORD told Moses He would bring Israel out of Egypt. And forgot when the LORD said Pharaoh will not let Israel go.

Exodus 5:20-23;

This thing of genocide of all the males of the Hebrews, and keep safe the females for the Egyptians males, who would rid the world of the Hebrews nation, however the Hebrew nation is no trouble to other nations, it is the LORD GOD of Israel; He's the GOD in whom other nations do not want to humble themselves too, nor do they want to serve Him, because It is written, Be ye Holy: for I am Holy.

I Peter 1:16.

The Holy Spirit the Spirit of truth has given to His servant in these last days, revelation into the Holy Scripture for all nations.

Here in Exodus chapter six we will know the truth of the name LORD by the Holy Spirit, the Spirit of truth.

Then the LORD said unto Moses, now shalt thou see what I will do to Pharaoh: for with a strong hand shall he let them go, and with a strong hand shall he drive them out of his land.

Exodus 6:1.

Beloved, We need to prepare our heart for this truth that is needful in these last days.

SECTION FOURTEEN THRU FIFTEEN

In this sixth section of reading we come to the most interesting truth in all scripture when Moses is told by Almighty GOD, the GOD of Abraham, Isaac, and Jacob; that He is the LORD; Sovereign Ruler over all creation. The Holy Spirit said that the name Jehovah is not the name for LORD in all the Bible. Anyone might say the name Jehovah is in my Bible. However, Beloved, the name Jehovah is not a name of GOD the Father, GOD the Son, or GOD the Holy Spirit. Not in the heavens will you find this name Jehovah. The Holy Spirit says the name Jehovah is not an Holy name, because the name LORD is Holy.

I AM THE LORD!

And GOD spake unto Moses, and said unto him, I am the LORD.

Exodus 6:2.

The name LORD, means the Sovereign One, The Ruler of heaven of heavens, and earth, and beneath the earth. I am Omnipotent, all powerful, I am Omniscient all knowing, I am Omnipresent, all present, and I Am GOD, ELOHIM, all I Am and all I manifest Myself to be, I Am The LORD, and I Am Holy, says The LORD.

And I appeared unto Abraham, unto Isaac, and unto Jacob, by the name of GOD ALMIGHTY, but by My name LORD was I not known to them.

Exodus 6:3.

He made known His ways unto Moses, His acts unto the children of Israel.

Psalm 103:7.

In my Bible where this scripture reads Exodus 6:3, and I appeared unto Abraham, unto Isaac, and unto Jacob, by the name of GOD ALMIGHTY, but by My name Jehovah was I not known to them.

This name Jehovah that the LORD said to Abraham, Isaac, and Jacob did not know Him by the name Jehovah, and rightly so because Jehovah is not the LORD'S name.

When I read this verse of scripture, Exodus 6:3, the Holy Spirit said to me there is none of the Holy Godhead named Jehovah. This name Jehovah is a popular name, and the name doesn't reach heaven, because the Holy Spirit, the Spirit of truth says, that GOD the Father, GOD the Son, and GOD the Holy Spirit of all the Holy Godhead does not respond to this name Jehovah.

Moses, the servant would not tell all generation pass, present, or future a false name for the LORD. Moses did not use any of the names of the gods from Egypt. Moses only gave to the people of GOD, the name that the LORD GOD gave him.

I am the LORD: that is My name: and My glory will I not give to another, neither My praise to graven images.

Isaiah 42:8.

Behold, the former things are come to pass, and new things do I declare: before they spring forth I tell you of them.

Isaiah 42:9.

I, even I, am the LORD; and beside Me there is no savior.

Isaiah 43:11.

That they may know from the rising of the sun, and from the west, that there is none beside Me. I am the LORD, and there is none else.

Isaiah 45:6.

Tell ye, and bring them near; yea, let them take counsel together: who hath declared this from ancient time? Who hath told it from that time? Have not I the LORD? And there is no GOD else beside Me; a just GOD and a Savior; there is none beside Me.

Look unto Me, and be ye saved, all the ends of the earth: for I am GOD, and there is none else.

Isaiah 45:21-22.

Remember the former things of old: for I am GOD, and there is none else; I am GOD, and there is none like Me.

Declaring the end from the beginning, and from ancient times the things that are not yet done, saying, My counsel shall stand, and I will do all My pleasure:

Isaiah 46:9-10.

For Mine own sake, even for Mine sake, will I do it; for how should My name be polluted? And I will not give My glory unto another.

Isaiah 48:11.

The Holy Spirit says at no time did the LORD call Himself Jehovah, nor did the LORD tell anyone His name was Jehovah God, in this world nor in the world to come.

I AM THE LORD!

Pharaoh and all of the Egyptians did not believe that there was a GOD of the Hebrews. They, the Egyptians was guilty of worshipping the creature rather then the Creator, who is blessed for ever. Amen.

Romans 1:21.

Professing themselves to be wise, they became fools.

Romans 1:22.

And changed the glory of the uncorruptible GOD into an image made like to corruptible man, and to birds, and four footed beasts, and creeping things.

Romans 1:23.

Our LORD JESUS CHRIST spoke these words to his Jewish audience in Matthews 12:29-Or else how can one enter into a strong man's house, and spoil his goods, except he first bind the strong man? And then he will spoil his house.

And the LORD made Moses a god to Pharaoh, and Aaron thy brother shall be thy prophet.

Exodus 7:1.

The LORD commanded Moses and Aaron to tell Pharaoh let the children of Israel go, and I will harden Pharaoh's heart, and multiply My signs and My wonders in the land of Egypt.

But Pharaoh shall not hearken unto you, that I may lay My hand upon Egypt, and bring forth Mine armies, and My children of Israel, out of the land of Egypt by great judgments.

And the Egyptians shall I know that I am the LORD, when I stretch forth Mine hand upon Egypt, and bring out the children of Israel from among them.

Exodus 7:3-5.

When the LORD told Moses and Aaron when they go before Pharaoh and he ask for a miracle, Exodus 7:9. When Pharaoh shall speak unto you, saying, show a miracle for you: then thou shalt say unto Aaron, take thy rod, and cast it before Pharaoh, and it shall become a serpent. The LORD JESUS said when you enter a strong man's house, you bind the strong man and subdue his house.

Matthew 12:29.

SECTION SIXTEEN THRU SEVENTEEN

Here in section seven we see the good fight of faith, by Moses and Aaron in using their rod, the rod of GOD to defeat Satan and all the demons of Egypt. Because the GOD of Israel is proving to all the known world He is the LORD, the Sovereign Ruler over all creation.

I AM THE LORD!

Here in Exodus 7:12-For they cast down every man his rod, and they became serpents: but Aaron's rod swallowed up their serpents.

Beloved, here we see that Satan is defeated in all of Egypt, because here in Egypt of all the gods Satan was the one, that evil one that needed to be defeated. Satan known as that old serpent, which is the Devil, and Satan, and bound him a thousand years.

Revelations 20:2.

The servants of the LORD , when obeying the command of the LORD would see the fulfilledment of the many revelation of the awesomeness of the LORD at work, in keeping His covenant promises to Abraham, to Isaac, and to Jacob.

When Aaron rod became a serpent, and Pharaoh thought in his heart, this trick isn't so great. When Pharaoh's wise men of sorcerers, working their magic, with their enchantments, all their powers of darkness is being consumed by Aaron's serpent.

Exodus 7:10-12.

The LORD is all knowing, and since some of us realize this truth we are much better off than many others. When we trick ourselves in believing we can contend against the Almighty GOD, we have lost it all. Pharaoh King of Egypt believes he's got a chance to prove who he is before all of the Egyptians and the children of Israel, because he was known as a god in Egypt. But he is not the LORD GOD Almighty that rules over the heavens and the earth.

Religion doesn't work in the sight of the LORD GOD ALMIGHTY, religion is powerless in any form, so why would anyone want to be stuck in a state of unbelief all their lives. Pharaoh the King of Egypt and all of the Egyptian will try continually to be all they think to be. Someone has said that the god Ra, the Egyptian god is the most powerful of the gods of Egypt, this is not true of Ra, the god of Egypt, because Aaron's rod which was turned into a serpent, and swallowed up the serpents of the Egyptian magicians.

Our LORD JESUS CHRIST said it best concerning Satan: Ye are of your father the devil, and the lusts of your father ye will do, He was a murderer from the beginning, and abode not in the truth, because there is no truth in him. When he speaketh a lie, he speaketh of his own: for he is a liar, and the father of it.

John 8:44.

Satan, deceived our first parents in the garden of Eden.

Genesis 3:1-3.

We also see Satan provoking David to sin:

I Chronicles 21:1-3.

How art thou fallen from heaven, O Lucifer, son of the morning! How art thou cut down to the ground, which didst weaken the nations!

For thou hast said in thine heart I will ascend into heaven, I will exalt my throne above the stars of GOD: I will sit also upon the mount of the congregation, in the sides of the north:

I will ascend above the heights of the clouds; I will be like the Most High.

Yet thou shalt be brought down, to hell, to the sides of the pit.

Isaiah 14:12-15.

Apostle Paul to the Hebrews says it like this in Hebrews 12:2: Looking unto JESUS the author and finisher of our faith; who for the joy that was set before Him endured the cross, despising the shame and is set down at the right hand of the throne of GOD.

And Apostle Peter had this to say, Who His own self bore our sins in His own body on the tree, that we being dead to sins, should live into righteousness: by whose stripes ye were healed.

I Peter 2:24.

Now the LORD is greatly prepared to show the known world just how awesome the LORD really is, by proving to the Pharaoh, the King of Egypt, and all of the Egyptians, and all of the children of Israel, because, as the Almighty GOD told Moses no one had known Him by the name LORD.

I AM THE LORD!

Thus far we have seen the rod of Aaron become a serpent to consumed the serpents of the magicians of Egypt. Now we come to the LORD'S plagues upon all of Egypt.

The LORD speaks through David in Psalm 32:9. Be ye not as the horse, or as the mule, which have no understanding: whose mouth must be held in with bit and bridle, lest they come near unto thee.

Now we shall see how the LORD, instructs Moses and Aaron in continuing use of the rod. The rod of the LORD.

Before the LORD say to Moses and Aaron what to do, He tells them what to say to Pharaoh King of Egypt, His request of Pharaoh if he is willing to comply to GOD'S request, no, no, no, says Pharaoh, because his heart is harden continually by the LORD GOD of Israel.

This first of the LORD'S plague is the plague of blood. There are ten plagues from the LORD that He will use to get and keep the attention of all Egypt.

The LORD GOD of the Hebrews tells Moses and Aaron, tell Pharaoh who I Am, and tell him My request, and with the rod in your hand do all I have commanded you to do.

SECTION EIGHTEEN THRU TWENTY

In this section of reading we see the awesomeness of GOD'S armies against His enemies for the sake of His glory. While GOD moves Moses and Aaron with the rod in Egypt. GOD only uses ten plagues to subdue the ten gods of the Egyptians.

I AM THE LORD!

The LORD GOD of the Hebrews says let My people go, that they may serve Me.

All the plagues from the LORD is used to prove His Sovereign power and His Sovereign authority over all of His creation.

I AM THE LORD !

This is the start of the ten plagues from the LORD, which is the plague of blood.

Exodus 7:17-19.

Since the Nile River it-self was a god to the ancient Egyptians. This plague from the LORD killed all living in the Nile River, such as fish, crocodile, and "etc."

The Egyptian magicians by their enchantments were able to turn water into blood, and there were blood throughout all the land of Egypt.

The rod of the LORD, in the hand of Aaron prove to be more powerful than the enchantments of Egypt magicians.

The LORD GOD of the Hebrews speak to Moses, and say go to Pharaoh and tell him, let My people go, that they may serve Me. And if Pharaoh refuse to let them go, I will strike all thy borders with frogs. This is the second plague from the LORD against the god or goddess of the Egyptians. Exodus 8:11-13-tells of the plague of the frogs for all the Egyptian to enjoy, and have a different kind of pet for themselves and their little ones.

Here is a list of some of the gods and goddess of the ancient Egyptians: There is, Ra of Re, Atum, Khnum, Apopis, Ptah, Apis, Isis Osiris, Aten, Heaut, Nut, Ged, Ma'at and Seth. The LORD'S quest is to defeat the first top ten of the Egyptians gods or goddesses, to prove He is the LORD.

The LORD said unto Moses, Say unto Aaron, Stretch out thy rod, and smite the dust of the land, that it may become lice throughout all the land of Egypt.

This is the third plague of the LORD. Exodus 8:16-19. Beloved, the lice was not lice, the translator got it wrong. The insects were fleas which came out of the dust of the ground. And the Egyptians with their enchantments could not bring from the dust of the ground fleas as the LORD GOD of Israel had done.

The magicians told Pharaoh, that it was the finger of GOD: when revelation came to the unbeliever concerning the awesomeness of GOD, certainly a believer should know for sure of the awesomeness of GOD.

Speaking of the finger of GOD, we find these words in Exodus 31:18. And He gave unto Moses, when He Had made an end of communing with him upon mount Sinai, two tables of testimony, tables of stone, written with the finger of GOD.

When we talk about how we know the LORD for oneself we see in John 8:6, This they said, tempting Him, that they might have to accuse Him. But JESUS stooped down, and with His finger wrote on the ground, as though He heard them not.

I AM THE LORD!

Moses and Aaron the servants of the LORD, that the plagues of the LORD is over powering the gods of Egypt. The fourth plague here in Exodus 8:20-29, the swarms of flies shall be upon all of the Egyptians, in their homes, on all the ground. However, the flies will not be in Goshen where My people are, and I will separate My people, form your people the Egyptians. Now Pharaoh ask Moses and Aaron to go sacrifice to the LORD your GOD for three days, don't go far, and return to me, and while you are there for the sacrifice intercede on my behalf to the GOD of Israel.

This fifth plague is the plague upon all cattle, horses, mules, camels, oxen, and upon sheep belonging to all the Egyptians, but none of the cattle, nor any of the livestock of Israel will be effected by the plague of death on all Egypt livestock.

Exodus 9:1-6.

The LORD GOD is really the ultimate in getting the attention of ancient Egypt. This sixth plague from the LORD upon all the Egyptians could be avoided my letting the LORD'S peoples go as requested. Pharaoh knows how to deal with Almighty GOD, if he has to use all of his body parts to prove it. Really? Exodus 9:8-12. The LORD told Moses and Aaron to get handfuls of ashes of the furnace, and stand before Pharaoh; sprinkled it up toward heaven; and it became a boil breaking forth with blains upon man, and upon beast. This plagues is sores, bluster, and boils, upon man and breast. On the body of all the magicians, the Egyptians, and Pharaoh was all these boils, blisters, and sores. Pharaoh, heart is hardened by the LORD GOD because the LORD is Omniscience, all knowing, by now any thinking person would give up, but not a demon possessed person whom Satan control can't give up.

I AM THE LORD!

Continuing in chapter nine, the LORD tell Moses, to go early in the morning to speak to Pharaoh, and tell him that the LORD GOD of the Hebrews, Let My people go, that they may serve Me. Exodus 9:13-26. This seventh plague by the LORD upon all of Egypt, the plague of hail. Listen what the LORD said to Pharaoh, the King of Egypt, for I will at this time send all My plague upon thine heart, and upon thy servants and upon thy people, that thou mayest know that there is none like Me in all the earth.

For now I will stretch out My hand, that I may smite thee and thy people with pestilence; and thou shalt be cut off from the earth.

And in very deed for this cause have I raised thee up, for to show in thee My people; and that My name may be declared through out all the earth.

I AM THE LORD!

In Exodus 9:27-And Pharaoh sent, and called for Moses and Aaron, and said unto them, I have sinned this time; the LORD is righteous, and I and my people are wicked.

To day in our churches we would conclude this is a form of repentance, it is not repentance. Paul says in 2nd Timothy 3:5-Having a form of godliness, but denying the power, thereof: from such turn away.

I AM THE LORD!

These plague of the LORD was not in an instance, it appear sometime was given for the Egyptians to recover from the devastation of all the plague from the LORD.

Here in Exodus 10:3-19-And Moses and Aaron came into Pharaoh, and said unto him, thus said the LORD GOD of the Hebrews, How long wilt thou refuse to humble thyself before Me? Let MY people go, that they may serve Me.

This plague of the Locusts will be so devastating for all the Egyptians that they may know that I Am The LORD! Pharaoh, calls for Moses and Aaron that they might intercede for the King and all Egypt, to be forgive for their stubbornness toward the LORD your GOD.

In Exodus 10:20-But the LORD hardened Pharaoh's heart, so that he would not let the children of Israel go. This was the eighth plague.

Now we see the ninth plague here in Exodus 10:21-29, it record the plague of darkness in all the land of the Egyptians, even darkness which may be felt. And Moses stretched forth his hand toward heaven: and there was a thick darkness in all the land of Egypt three days. Beloved, when the darkness is this thick that you can not see your hand before your face, it is darkness at its worse.

And the LORD, said to Moses, yet will I bring one plague more upon Pharaoh, and upon Egypt: afterwards he will let you go hence; when he shall let you go, he shall surely thrust you out hence altogether.

Exodus 11:1-10.

This is the tenth plague of the firstborn of all the Egyptians, from the firstborn of man and the firstborn of beasts.

And the LORD GOD promised Abraham a child, a man child. And the LORD told Abraham that He would make a great nations of him, Kings of people shall be by Sarah, his wife. Genesis 17:15-16.

SECTION TWENTY ONE THRU TWENTY TWO

This is the section of reading we see the LORD establish the covenant Passover; because the GOD of Abraham, Isaac, and Jacob is making the children of Israel a nation, before He bring them out of Egypt, blessed for the promise land.

I AM THE LORD!

Abraham at this time was childless, so the LORD made a covenant with Abraham and He promised that He would bless him and his seed after him, and all his seeds would be bless.

Genesis 15.

In Genesis 15:13-And He said unto Abram, know of a surety that thy, seed shall be a stranger in a land that is not theirs, and shall serve them: and they shall afflict them four hundred years:

V 14-And also that nation, whom they shall serve, will I judge: and afterward shall they come out with great substance.

Promised, kept by the LORD to Abraham, here in Exodus 11:2-Speak now in the ears of the people, and let every man received of his neighbor, and every woman of her neighbor, jewels of silver and jewels of gold.

I AM THE LORD!

Here in Exodus 12th chapter the LORD give Moses specific instruction to prepare all of Israel for the Passover celebration, because of the awesome power of deliverance that the LORD GOD of the Hebrews is about to perform for all of Israel, and to show before the face of the Egyptians, I AM THE LORD!

The LORD said to Moses and Aaron. This month shall be unto you the beginning of months: it shall be the first month of the year to you.

The LORD declares a new life, a new beginning, a new hope, and a new land, that all Israel could call home, the land , that flow with milk and honey, the land that is blessed by the LORD GOD of hosts. No where in this new journey for all of Israel that the name of the LORD is Jehovah, because the Holy Spirit of the Holy Godhead, says there is none of the Godhead named Jehovah.

I AM THE LORD!

When the LORD establish the covenant Passover for all of Israel to remember the LORD awesome power in all of Egypt, and also in, Remembrance of Me! The first ten days of the first month, Israel was to put up a lamb or goat of one year old, a male without blemish and keep it up, which is off the ground until the fourteenth day of the same month. All of the whole assembly of the congregation of Israel shall kill it in the evening. Take the blood, put in on the two side posts and on the upper door post of the houses, where you eat it. The male lamb or goat must be roast with fire, with his head and legs, eaten with unleavened bread, and bitter herbs.

Psalms 34:20.

The male lamb of goat must not to be boiled nor eaten raw, only roast with fire. This is none other than an Holy Barbecue. None of the Passover meal was not to remain until morning, but to burn in the fire.

All of Israel was to eat the Passover meal in an hurry, fully dressed, shoes on their feet, staff in their hands, it is the LORD'S Passover. In the first month, on the fourteenth day of the month, at evening, you shall eat unleavened bread, until the one and twentieth day of the month at evening. Seven days shall there be no leaven found in your houses: for whosoever eateth that which is leavened, even that soul shall be cut off from the congregation of Israel, whether he be a stranger, or born in the land.

I AM THE LORD!

During this first Passover celebration, that the angels of the LORD, that once He saw the blood, He would Passover, However if He did not see the blood on the door posts of the houses, all of the firstborn of Egypt died, whether in Pharaoh house are of his servants behind the mill, or the magicians, of the Egyptians, all the firstborn of man and of beasts was dead in all the houses of Egypt. All the houses of Israel had the blood of the Lamb of GOD who taketh away the sins of the world.

John 1:29.

I AM THE LORD!

There were in the last few verse of chapter twelve certain restriction for those who were not of the children of Israel who might want to partake of the LORD'S Passover meal.vs43-49.

In chapter thirteen of Exodus, the LORD spoke to Moses, saying, Sanctify unto Me all the firstborn, whatsoever openeth the womb among the children of Israel, both man and of beast: it is Mine!

The Exodus of Israel out of Egypt was the month Abib, the beginning of spring, between April and May of our months: v4.

So the LORD led the children of Israel and the stranger, which were the mixed multitude, out of the house of bondage, out of the land of Egypt. Verse twenty two says, He took not away the pillar of the cloud by day, nor the pillar of fire by night, from before the people.

The LORD GOD of the Hebrews knew that Israel would fill safe and protected with the mountains on both side of them, with the Red Sea in front of them, and the angel of GOD with fire to secure their well being, and also to prevent Israel from returning back to Egypt. Here is this fourteenth chapter of Exodus we see the LORD at work on the hardening of Pharaoh's heart, for He tells Moses that Pharaoh the King of Egypt did not want to let Israel go so He must this one last time cause Pharaoh to pursue after the children of Israel, that I will be honored by Pharaoh, and all his host; that the Egyptians may know that I AM THE LORD!

SECTION TWENTY THREE THRU THIRTY FIVE

In section number ten we will be blessed if we look to GOD for a better understanding how He work in blessing all that would thank Him for all His goodness in their lives.

These titles to the LORD'S name is right, according to the Holy Spirit. So be blessed in your yes to the LORD GOD ALMIGHTY. These commentaries are for our edification.

I AM THE LORD!

And the angel of GOD, which went before the camp of Israel, removed and went behind them; and the pillar of the cloud went from before their face, and stood behind them: The angel of GOD protecting the children of Israel from the Egyptian army.

What shall we then say to these things? If GOD be for us, who can be against us?

Romans 8:31.

In verse 21, and Moses stretched out his hand over the sea; and the LORD caused the sea to go back by a strong east wind all that night, and made the sea dry land, and the waters were divided.

And all of Israel went through the midst of the sea on dry land, and the Egyptians pursued after them, however the LORD was fighting for Israel that day and finally all of Egypt knew for themselves how awesome the LORD GOD of the Hebrews is in subduing Israel enemies by drowning all the Egyptians that came into the midst of the sea.

Exodus 14:22-31.

Many have said that when praises go up, then blessing come down. We see here how Moses and the children of Israel giving the LORD GOD thanks for what He has done for them, how He blessed them by destroying their enemies, and preserving their souls alive, Praise the LORD.

Exodus 15:1-21.

Often time the man of GOD, which is Moses, having to deal with people that believe, but help my unbelief. It seem as if Israel constantly doubted in the awesomeness of GOD ALMIGHTY. They need water, the water is bitter, they turn against Moses, and at the same time turn against Almighty GOD, all because the water is bitter. These people just witness how the LORD worked the waters of the Red Sea, so this bitter waters is not to hard for the LORD.

Exodus 15:22-27.

The children of Israel is going to be tested by GOD Almighty, so they will know to obey the voice of the LORD.

Note: In Exodus fifteen chapter verse twenty six, the LORD said, if thou wilt diligently hearken to the voice of the LORD thy GOD, and wilt do that which is right in His sight, and wilt give ear to His commandments, and keep all His statutes, I will put none of these diseases upon thee, which I have brought upon the Egyptians: for I AM THE LORD that healeth thee.

This is the LORD who heals you or me. El-Rophi the LORD who heals you YHWH, is the LORD who heals thee. This is the only LORD GOD who is capable or able to heal from all sicknesses, and from all diseases.

In the life of King Ahaziah over Israel in Samaria, how he fell down through the crossed bars of his upper chamber that was in Samaria, and was sick. Sent his servants to enquire of Baalzebub the god of Ekron whether he shall recover of this disease. The King's servants left to go to ask for the King, will he recover? However , the LORD called His servant Elijah and told him to tell the servants of the King. Thou shalt not come down from that bed on which thou art gone up, but shalt surely die. Elijah delivered the message just as he was told by the LORD, and the King got the message, however the King concluded that the message was from Elijah the Tishbite, but in fact the word was from the LORD, El-Rophi, the LORD who can heal you.

2nd Kings 1:1-17.

Our LORD JESUS in teaching His disciple how to be as their master, here in Matthew 10:25-It is enough for the disciple that he be as his master, and the servant as his lord. If they have called the master of the house Beelzebub, how much more shall they call them of his household? So, we see here how our LORD called Satan, Baalzebub.

JESUS say in Matthew 12:27-28.-In verse twenty seven-And if I by Baalzebub cast out devils, by whom do your children cast them out? Therefore they shall be your judges.

As we continue in verse twenty eight-But if I cast out devils by the Spirit of GOD, then the kingdom of GOD is come unto you.

There is no healing in Baalzebub, the god of Ekron of the Phillistine. There is healing from the LORD GOD of the Hebrews.

Here in the book of Isaiah 53:5-But He was wounded for our transgressions, He was bruised for our iniquities: the chastisement of our peace was upon Him: and with His stripes we are healed. This two-fold healing by the blood of the Lamb of GOD, healing from our sin, and healing for all sickness and for all disease.

Apostle Peter says it like this in I Peter 2:24-Who His own self bore our sins in His own body on the tree, that we, being dead to sins, should live unto righteousness: by whose stripes ye were healed.

JESUS CHRIST says of Himself in the mouth of Matthew, in Matthew gospel, Matthew 4:23-And JESUS went about all Galilee, teaching in their synagogues, and preaching the gospel of the kingdom, and healing all manner of sickness and all manner of disease among the people. This is none other than El-Rophi, the LORD who healeth thee. YHWH, the LORD who healeth thee. I AM THE LORD. El-Rophi, the LORD my healer.

NOTE: Here in Genesis chapter seventeen, beginning at verse one; And when Abram was ninety years old and nine, the LORD appeared to Abram, and said to him, I AM THE ALMIGHTY GOD; walk before Me, and be thou perfect, El-Shaddai, the LORD GOD ALMIGHTY.

Now the LORD tells Abram that He is ALMIGHTY GOD, notice, Abram didn't tell the LORD who He was. Just as the LORD spoke to

Moses in Exodus 6:3-And I appeared unto Abraham, unto Isaac, and unto Jacob, by the name of GOD ALMIGHTY, but by My name LORD was I not known to them.

So the Hebrew name for ALMIGHTY GOD is El-Shaddai, the LORD GOD ALMIGHTY.

The LORD GOD made a covenant with Abram, and promise him, he would be a father of many nations. He told Abram his name would no more be Abram, but Abraham, meaning a father of many nations, you will be exceeding fruitful, and I will make nations of thee, and King shall come out of thee.

And I will establish My covenant between Me and thee and the seed after thee in their generations for an everlasting covenant, after thee. And ye shall circumcise the flesh of your foreskin; and it shall be a token of the covenant between Me and you.

All male born in your house or bought with thy money shall be circumcised, and My covenant shall be in your flesh for an everlasting covenant.

And GOD said to Abraham, As for Sarai thy wife, thou shalt not call her name Sarai, but Sarah shall be her name.

And I will bless her, and give thee a son also of her; yea, I will bless her, and she shall be a mother of nations; Kings of people shall be of her.

When we look into the sacred writing of Holy Scripture we should rejoice in the LORD for the awesome acts of wisdom and power, rather to laughed with fear and with unbelief, the LORD said I AM ALMIGHTY GOD, My covenant is with thee, and thou shalt be a father of many nations.

In Genesis chapter Twenty one, as we look at verse one, and the LORD visited Sarah as He had said, and the LORD did unto Sarah as He had spoken. Verse two, for Sarah conceived, and bare Abraham a son in his old age, at the set time of which GOD had spoken to him.

The LORD had work to do in the bodies of his servants Abraham and Sarah. Apostle Paul says this truth in Romans 4:19-And being not weak in faith, he considered not his own body now dead, when he was about an hundred years old, neither yet the deadness of Sarah's womb:

The baby Isaac is circumcised the eight day, for the covenant blessing of promise, because this baby brought laughter to two old souls of faith.

At the age of twelve, Abraham was told to take Isaac and offer him to GOD on the mountain that He would show him. This Abraham's only son, so Abraham obeys the voice of the LORD. Someone has said that the morning Abraham took Isaac his only son to be a sacrifice to the LORD, that Sarah had a heart attack and died, not seeing Isaac her only son again.

The Holy Spirit says that Isaac was twelve years old, when Abraham was commanded to offer his only son Isaac as a sacrifice to the LORD, thus Sarah lived twenty five more years with Isaac her only son, and with her husband Abraham.

In Genesis chapter twenty three, Sarah lived to be hundred and seven and twenty years old: these were the years of the life of Sarah. Her son Isaac would have been 37 years when Sarah died.

Paul's says in Romans tenth chapter verse seventeen, So then faith cometh by hearing, and hearing by the word of GOD.

Here in Genesis chapter twenty two, Abraham, the father of faith, speaks faith. Abraham believe that the LORD GOD want him to sacrifice his only son on mount Moriah. Abraham speaks faith to his young servant, he say to them the lad and I will go up on the mount and worship and come again. Abraham tells his son, his only son Isaac, when he ask where is the offering for the burnt offering, faith speaks, GOD will provide His own sacrifice. Abraham prepare the wood, the fire and his son his only son.

And we hear, as did Abraham to the voice of covenant promise, do not harm the lad, your only son, behind you is a ram caught in a thicket by his horn: and Abraham went and took the ram and offered him up for a burnt offering instead of his son, And Abraham called the place El-jireh, the LORD GOD our provider. The Holy Spirit continue to say of the Holy Godhead there is none of the Godhead named Jehovah, and none of the Godhead will never respond to the name of Jehovah, past, present or in the future in the heavens. I AM THE LORD!

Apostle Paul says in Galatians 3:29-And if ye be CHRIST'S, then are ye Abraham's seed; and heirs according to the promise. This is the same El-Shaddai that made a covenant with Abraham that He might bless all nations through his Seed. Galatians 3:16.

I AM THE LORD!

El-jireh, the LORD GOD our provider, is here in Matthew 6:33-But seek ye first the kingdom of GOD, and His righteousness; and all these things shall be added unto you. Every thing you and I have need of El-jireh is able to provide. Apostle Paul says it like this; But my GOD shall supply all your need according to His riches in glory by CHRIST JESUS, Philippians 4:19. In Hebrew, He is the LORD Adonay, the LORD of Israel.

I AM THE LORD!

NOTE: El-nissi, the LORD GOD My Banner. In Exodus seventeenth chapter verse fifteen it reads, And Moses build an alter, and called the name of it El-nissi: the LORD GOD my Banner.

In verse sixteen Moses says, for he said, because the LORD hath sworn that the LORD will have war with Amalek from generation to generation.

El-nissi is our battle Axe. I will go before thee, and make the crooked places straight:

I will break in pieces the gates of brass, and cut in sunder the bars of iron: This is one of the promises made by the LORD to His anointed Cyrus, the future King of Babylon.

Some one hundred fifty to one hundred sixty years into the future, before his birth. The LORD promises that King Cyrus would be victorious in defeating the King of Babylon.

Isaiah 45:1-7.

Again this is El-nissi, the LORD GOD my Banner. King David found help and encouragement in El-nissi, the LORD my Banner. In Psalm 28:7-8- The LORD is my strength and my shield: my heart trusted in Him, and I am helped: therefore my heart greatly rejoiceth; and with my song will I praise Him.

The LORD is their strength, and He is the saving strength of His anointed.

Thou are my hiding place and my shield: I hope in Thy word.

Psalm 119:114.

My goodness, and my fortess; my high tower, and my deliverer, my shield, and He in whom I trust; who subdueth my people under me.

El-nissi, the LORD GOD our Banner is all these acts of protecting us, and defending us, and blessing us with more of who the LORD GOD of Israel is in His divine present for His anointed servants.

Apostle Paul speaks of LORD Adonay, El-nissi, the LORD my Banner in Hebrews 12:2-Looking unto JESUS the author and finisher of our faith;

who for the joy that was set before Him endured the cross, despising the shame, and is set down at the right hand of the throne of GOD. I AM THE LORD!

NOTE: El-Roi, the LORD GOD of Israel Who Sees me.

Hagar in her attempt to flee from Sarai her mistress, being with child, she was found by an angel of the LORD by a fountain of water in the wilderness, by the fountain of water in the wilderness, by the fountain in the way to Shur. The angel asks Hagar two question, where are you coming from? And where are you going? Hagar answer to the first of the two question is clear, she says she was fleeing from the face of Sarai her mistress, but she do not know where she is going. The angel of the LORD tells Hagar return to thy mistress, submit yourself to her. And the LORD said I will multiply thy seed exceedingly, that it shall not be numbered for multitude. And the angel of the LORD said unto her, Behold, thou art with child, and shalt bear a son, and shalt call his name Ishmael because the LORD hath heard thy affliction.

And he will be a wild man; his hand will be against every man, and every man's hand against him; and he shall dwell in the presence of all his brethren.

And she called the name of the LORD that spake unto her, Thou GOD seest me; for she said, Have I also here looked after Him that seeth me? Genesis 16:6-13.

In the Hebrew is El-Roi, the LORD GOD of Israel who sees me.

When Hagar return to Sarai and Abraham as the angel of the LORD commanded her, she knew that she knew the very same Almighty GOD as Abraham and Sarah knew.

This El-Roi is also the Shepherd of our souls. When King David penned the words to Psalm twenty three verses one, The LORD is my shepherd, I shall not want. Now the word want is the word for prosperity, it means to lack nothng. El-Roi, promised Hagar in Genesis chapter sixteen to prosper her descendants. Here in Genesis seventeen chapter verse two. And I will make My covenant between Me and thee, and will multiply thee exceedingly. Abraham was rich, very rich in cattle, in silver, and in gold.

Genesis 13:2.

In John's gospel concerning JESUS CHRIST, in chapter ten verses fourteen and fifteen these are those words.

I am the good shepherd, and know My sheep, and am known of Mine.

As the Father knoweth Me, even so know I the Father: and I lay down My life for the sheep.

What do you suppose a sheep should do to show their appreciation for our Shepherd who has giving His life for us, that we might have life and the abundant life?

John 10:10.

My sheep hear My voice, and I know them, and they follow Me.

John 10:27.

Now Abraham had two sons, Ishmael and Isaac. Ishmael the son of a bondwoman, and Isaac, the son of promise. Sarah became tired of the mocking of Hagar and her son Ishmael, so she told Abraham to cast them out from her, so Abraham was hurt because of the separation, but the LORD GOD of Israel told Abraham, Sarah was right, put them out. Abraham gave Hagar and Ishmael his son a bottle of water and bread and sent them away, and they wandered in the wilderness of Beesheba. The bread and the water was used up, and there was no more to eat or drink.

Hagar, did not want to see her only son perish before her face, so she put her son under a shrubs and left him fearing the worst, and she begin go cry with a loud voice. GOD (Elohim) heard the voice of Ishmael in prayer for help, for he knew the Almighty GOD of the Hebrews, because he is Hebrew the first son of Abraham.

Genesis 17:22-27.

And Ishmael knew he could call on the LORD GOD of Israel, because his mother Hagar had told him about El-Roi, the GOD who sees me. Listen what the GOD (Elohim) of Israel is saying to twelve princes of Ishmael, And GOD heard the voice of the lad;and the angel of GOD called to Hagar out of heaven, and said unto her, What aileth thee, Hagar? Fear not; for GOD hath heard the voice of the lad, where he is.

Arise, lift up the lad, and hold him in thine hand; for I will make him a great nation.

And GOD opened her eyes, and she saw a well of water; and she went, and filled the bottle with water, and gave the lad drink.

And GOD was with the lad; and he grew, and dwelt in the wilderness and became an archer.

If Abraham, Isaac, Jacob, and Ishmael, called on the GOD Almighty, the LORD GOD of the Hebrews, and these four servants of Almighty GOD got answer to their prayers, then we must consider our thoughts and action, from those thoughts to be sure it is Almighty GOD who is moving us in His will, and not our will. I AM THE LORD.

Genesis 21:10-21.

NOTE: Now we turn our attention to El-Tsidikenu, the LORD GOD our Righteousness.

Jeremiah 23:6, In His days Judah shall be saved, and Israel shall dwell safely, and this is His name whereby He shall be called, The LORD our Righteousness.

This is El-Taisikenu, the LORD our Righteousness.

In the Psalm of David, David understands the righteousness of GOD in one's life.

Blessed is he whose transgression is forgiven, whose sin is covered.

Blessed is the man unto whom the LORD imputed not iniquity, and in whose spirit there is no guile.

Psalm 32:1-2.

That word blessed is the word that means that the divine favor of the LORD is upon you, to give you peace and comfort after the LORD has blessed you with Himself. Thus receiving the righteousness of the LORD. To have fellowship with the GOD of glory is awesome with in itself, and to have a sense of worth given by GOD to His creature is a blessing within itself.

For GOD so loved the world that He gave His only begotten Son, that whoever believe on Him, should not perish but have everlasting life.

John 3:16.

And the glory which Thou gavest Me I have given them; that they may be one, even as We are one.

John 17:22

I in them, and Thou in Me, that they may be made perfect in one; and that the world may know that Thou hast, sent Me, and hast loved them, as Thou hast loved Me.

John 17:23.

Apostle Paul address this issue of righteousness through faith. For what saith the scripture? Abraham believed GOD, and it was counted unto him for righteousness.

Romans 4:3.

For the promise, that he should be the heir of the world, was not to Abraham, or of his seed, through the law, but through the righteousness of faith.

Romans 4:13.

Now it was not written for his sake alone, that it was in imputed to him;

But for us also, to whom it shall be imputed, if we believe on Him that raised up JESUS our LORD from the dead;

Who was delivered for our offenses and was raised again for our justification.

Romans 4:23-25. El-Tsidikenu, The LORD Our Righteousness. I AM THE LORD!

NOTE: El-Shalom, The LORD GOD Our Peace and Prosperity.

Then Gideon built an altar there unto the LORD, and called it El-Shalom: unto this day it is yet in Ophrah of the Abiezrites.

Judges 6:24.

The Prophet Isaiah speak about the peace of GOD, in Isaiah twenty six chapter verses three and four.

Thou wilt keep him in perfect peace; whose mind is stayed on Thee: because he trusteth in Thee.

Trust ye in the LORD for ever: for in the LORD is everlasting strength:

Isaiah 26:3-4.

In the Hebrew tongue the LORD is called Adonay, which means LORD.

El-Shalom, the LORD GOD our Peace and Prosperity.

Our blessed Savior and LORD JESUS CHRIST says of Himself: Peace I leave with you, My peace I give unto you: not as the world giveth, give I unto you. Let not your heart be troubled, neither let it be afraid.

John 14:27.

When our LORD JESUS says, "give I unto you", in this verse, He is saying for an absolute surety, there is no fear couple with the peace He is giving, because His peace is Himself.

Adonay Shalom, the LORD is our Peace and Prosperity.

When the church, the body of CHRIST put into practice the simplicity of the word of GOD, then we will receive from and by the Holy Spirit the full revelation of the word of GOD.

Pray for the peace of Jerusalem: they shall prosper that love thee.

Peace be within thy walls, and prosperity within thy palaces.

Psalm 122:6-7.

The LORD spake unto Moses, saying, Speak unto Aaron and unto his sons, saying, On this wise ye shall bless the children of Israel, saying unto them.

The LORD bless thee, and keep thee:

The LORD make His face shine upon thee, and be gracious unto thee:

The LORD lift up His countenance upon thee, and give thee peace.

And they shall put My name upon the children of Israel; and I will bless them.

Numbers 6:22-27.

Apostle Peter speaks about the Priesthood of the believer in CHRIST JESUS our LORD, which every man of GOD that has a wife and family should take authority in exercising his anointed priesthood in their home. A husband and father should put his hands upon his wife head and bless her with words of blessing and encouragement, also pray for her safety and security.

The father of his family should lay hands on his children and bless them by praying for them for their safety and respect to those adults that are in authority. Length of days is in her right hand; and in her left hand riches and honor. Proverbs 3:16. I know this verse of scripture speaks about her, which is wisdom. Brethren, if this is true then receive the revelation of this verse of scripture, by asking the LORD for His divine favor upon every soul in your family.

I AM THE LORD!

Now, for the mother who do not have a husband, but have children and heads of their families, Mother's you can also lay your hands upon your children heads and pray for them asking the LORD blessing upon your children in every area of their life, upon every area of their living, and upon every area of their service to CHRIST JESUS our LORD. Our LORD JESUS says this: The thief cometh not, but for to steal, and to kill, and to destroy: I am come that they might have life, and that they might have it more abundantly!

John 10:10.

NOTE: Abraham the father of faith, in his victory over his enemies, and the enemies of his family. It was the victory that the Most High GOD gave unto Abram over his enemies. Genesis 14:18-24. El-Elyon. Hebrew.

We shall see how the Most High GOD blessed Abram in his faith walk with the LORD. It is believed that Melchizedek was none other than the pre-incarnate CHRIST.

When Abram told the King of Sodom, I have lift up mine hand unto the LORD, the Most High GOD, the possessor of heaven and earth. Abraham stood on the promises of Almighty GOD, and he knew that all that he had need of, the LORD, the Most High GOD would supply, because He was possessor of heaven and earth.

Abram had given to the LORD, his tithe of all.

Abraham, Isaac, and Jacob gave their tithe of all to the LORD. Here in Malachi chapter three, beginning in verse 6-12.

For I AM THE LORD, I change not; therefore ye sons of Jacob are not consumed.

Abraham said he had lift his hand to the LORD. He the LORD says He change not. This is the same LORD of Abraham, that Abraham honored by worshiping the LORD with his offering.

When we give of our treasury that the LORD has bless us to receive it in the first place we need to give honor to the LORD, for all His goodness, by giving our tithes and offering to the LORD at our local churches. That the spreading of the gospel of JESUS CHRIST our LORD in this earth realm, which is the death, burial, and resurrection of our LORD JESUS CHRIST.

Honor the LORD, with thy substance, and with the firstfruits of all thine increase.

Proverbs 3:9.

So shall thy barns be filled with plenty, and thy presses shall burst out with new wine.

Proverbs 3:10.

Upon the first day of the week let every one of you lay by him in store, as GOD hath prospered him, that there be no gatherings when I come.

I Corinthians 16:2.

Beloved, when we do not tithes our income there is a double curse upon us in verse nine. Further, the LORD says, if we tithe our income that He (the LORD of hosts) would rain out of the windows of heaven blessing, multiplied blessing, that we would not have room enough to contain them, Verse 10.

If anyone say to you that GOD is moving a window of blessing over you, because this is your season of blessing, remember faith come by hearing, and hearing by the word of GOD.

Romans 10:17.

But evil men and seducers shall wax worse and worse, deceiving, and begin deceived.

2nd Timothy 3:13.

For we ourselves also were sometimes foolish, disobedient, deceived, serving divers lusts and pleasures, living in malice and envy, hateful, and hating one another.

Titus 3:3.

The LORD of hosts says that He will rebuke the devourer for your sake; in other words, the LORD will not allow any insects, or animals or any disease destroy the things He has blessed you with; neither shall your vine cast her fruit before the time in the field, saith the LORD of hosts.

Your fruits and vegetables will not be pre-mature on the tree or vine they will come to full maturity for your families.

NOTE: In the prophesy of Ezekiel, chapter forty eight verse thirty five; It was round about eighteen thousand measures: and the name of the city from that day shall be, The LORD is there, which is El-Shammah, the LORD is there in the Hebrew tongue.

We can see in scripture the goodness of the LORD in all His doing when He bless with abundant blessing in hard time. In the twentieth six chapter of Genesis we see the covenant attributes of the LORD'S favor upon Isaac and his family in the midst of the Philistines, alone with a famine in the land.

The LORD told Isaac do not go down into Egypt; dwell in the land which I shall tell thee of: Beloved, El-Shammah is there, remember, the earth is the LORD'S and the fullness thereof; the world and they that dwell therein.

Psalm 24:1.

Wherever the sons and daughters of the LORD is El—Shammah is there.

This truth that the LORD spoke to Isaac, Isaac was to believe on the LORD that GOD would provide for Isaac and his family. The LORD said, Sojourn in this land, and I will be with thee, and will bless thee; for unto thee, and unto thy seed, I will give all these countries, and I will perform the oath which I sware unto Abraham thy father; El-Shamman, the LORD is there.

NOTE: Moses writes about Abraham as the LORD tells him what to record for future generation. Here in Genesis chapter twenty one verse thirty three, and Abraham planted a grove in Beersheba, and called there on the name of the LORD, the everlasting GOD.

The Everlasting GOD, in the Hebrew language is El-Olam, meaning, GOD is The Eternal One.

The Everlasting GOD, is the GOD of our past, He is the GOD of our present, and He is the GOD of our future.

Moses write again concerning the everlasting GOD, The eternal GOD is thy refuge, and underneath are the everlasting arms: and He shall thrust out the enemy from before thee; and shall say. Destroy them.

Deuteronomy 33:27.

King David in his psalm remembered how faithful the eternal GOD was in his time of trouble, The LORD shall reign for ever, even thy GOD, O ZION, unto all generations.

Praise ye the LORD.

Psalm 146:10.

I AM THE LORD!

NOTE: At the very start of these writing, the Holy Spirit instructed me in all my ways in obeying His direction. In Exodus, chapter six, where we begin to write about truth and righteousness. Let us again look at two verse of scripture that will help us now and in the future.

And GOD spake unto Moses, and said unto him, I AM THE LORD: Verse Two.

And I appeared unto Abraham, unto Isaac, and unto Jacob, by the name of GOD Almighty, but by My name Jehovah was I not known to them. Verse Three.

This is when the Holy Spirit spoke to His servant and said, there is none of the Holy Godhead named Jehovah, past, present, or ever in the future.

All of the children of Israel has never known Jehovah, nor ever will know Jehovah by the Holy Spirit, the Spirit of truth.

Someone wanted Israel and all creation to use this word Jehovah, which is a blaspheming name for the LORD GOD of Israel.

Many ministers from all backgrounds and denomination have put this word Jehovah into their religious practices.

The Holy Spirit, the Spirit of truth is saying that the name Jehovah is not the name of the LORD, nor is it for the LORD. Moses the servant of the LORD GOD Almighty would not pass on a name of the LORD, that was not His name. Because the name Jehovah is not a Hebrew word, nor is it written in the Hebrew language.

I AM THE LORD!

There is perhaps thousands of known languages in this world. The United Nations, has officially excepted only six of the known languages, for their purposes; English, French, Chinese, Arabia, Spanish, and Russian. At the U.N. whosoever will of other country with other languages will have to have a translator to translate the language in all U.N. meetings.

Like the United Nations, all the nations that are in agreement will unite in whatever the deciding decision might be that will have some kind of effect on other countries that were not members.

There is a great number of individual who would love to leave a legacy of their worth while in this life, that other may say I was here to serve.

Let's look at something of great interest, that we really need to give a great amount of consideration concerning the GOD of the Bible.

Do we really know who He is?

And did we really worship Him in spirit and in truth? John 4:24.

There is a false hood of thinking in the minds of many people who think that all is going to heaven my friends it's not true. Only the saved will go.

Romans 10:9-10.

The Church of CHRIST JESUS our LORD will be taken out of the world soon.

For the LORD Himself shall descend from heaven with a shout, with the voice of the archangel, and with the trump of GOD: and the dead in CHRIST shall rise first:

Then we which are alive and remain shall be caught up together with them in the clouds to meet the LORD in the air: and so shall we ever be with the LORD.

I Thessalonians 4:16-17.

After the church of CHRIST is our of the world, the antichrist will begin showing himself to be god in the temple of GOD.

2nd Thessalonians 2:4.

During the times of the antichrist, what happen to the gospel of JESUS CHRIST, the legacy that the Church left with those who heard, but did not believe the gospel.

John 15:23.

Remember: that at the name of JESUS every knee should bow, of things in heaven, and things in earth, and things under the earth:

SECTION THIRTY SIX THRU THIRTY EIGHT

In section number eleven note in Whom we need to put our faith and trust in; is the LORD JESUS CHRIST, our only Savior for the whole world.

John 3:16-17.

I AM THE LORD!

And that every tongue should confess that JESUS CHRIST is LORD, to the glory of GOD the Father.

Philippians 2:10-11.

In the book of Revelation chapter seven verse four thru eight;

And I heard the number of them which were sealed: and there were sealed an hundred and forty and four thousand of all the tribes of the children of Israel.

All nations on this earth has a language, some are problematic, and some languages just shouldn't be used. If we see in our languages or tongue that there is none of our words to match, the name LORD, like this word Jehovah is a concoction of some one who knew no better, than to try to force this name Jehovah to mean LORD.

In the prophetic book of Zechariah we find there words of truth for all:

Thus saith the LORD of hosts; In those days it shall come to pass; that ten men shall take hold out of all languages of the nations, even shall take hold of the skirt of him that is a Jew, saying, We will go with you: for we have heard that GOD is with you.

Zechariah 8:23.

Beloved, all nations will need to know the LORD GOD of the Hebrews, how about you?

I am the LORD, your Holy One, the creator of Israel, your King.

Isaiah 43:15.

And GOD spake unto Israel in the visions of the night, and said Jacob, Jacob, and he said, Here am I.

Genesis 46:2-4

And He said, I AM GOD, the GOD of thy father: fear not to go down into Egypt: for I will there make of thee a great nations.

I will go down with thee into Egypt: and I will also surely bring thee up again; and Joseph shall put his hand upon thine eyes.

Israel and all his family goes with the LORD down to Egypt (a type of the world) to become a nation of the LORD GOD of the Hebrews, in the midst of idol gods and false religion.

In these ancient times all nations served only the gods of their nation;

2nd Kings 17:25-36.

Moses served the LORD GOD faithfully. In Exodus chapter forty, verse sixteen.

Thus did Moses: according to all that the LORD commanded him, so did he.

Moses, the man of GOD, serve the LORD in all kinds of adverse situation, and he was obedient to the LORD no matter what the cost. We know that the LORD was with him through it all, and that is the promise of the LORD, certainly, I will be with thee: and this shall be a token unto thee, that I have sent thee: When thou hast brought forth Israel out of Egypt, ye shall serve GOD upon this mountains.

Exodus 3:12.

Moses never ever blaspheme that holy name LORD, as he stood in Egypt before all of Israel, and Pharaoh the King of the Egyptians, Moses said that the LORD GOD of the Hebrews hath sent me unto thee saying, Let My people go, that they may serve Me in the wilderness: and behold, hitherto thou wouldest not hear.

Exodus 7:16.

Beloved, just as all the known world doing the time and ministry of Moses, the people did not want to hear the very voice of the LORD GOD of Israel, however we think, or whatever language we speak there will come a time when we need to search for truth in this earth realm, for the truth of GOD'S word is here. Even the Spirit of truth; whom the world cannot receive, because it seeth Him not, neither knoweth Him: but ye know Him; for He dwelleth with you, and shall be in you.

John 14:17.

Beloved, we need to rely upon the Holy Spirit more often than none. These last days are days of worth, in other words we must make every day count for the cause of CHRIST and His Church. Every day should be a day of deliverance for some lost soul, that need a Savior and a LORD that will bless his or her life daily and forever.

And He said unto them, These are the words which I spake unto you, while I was yet with you, that all things must be fulfilled, which were written in the law of Moses, and in the prophets, and in the psalms, concerning Me. Luke 24:44. This is CHRIST JESUS our LORD: Genesis thru Malachi.

And of His fullness have all we received, and grace for grace.

For the law was given by Moses, but grace and truth came by JESUS CHRIST.

John 1:16-17.

How GOD anointed JESUS of Nazareth with the Holy Ghost and power: who went about doing good, and healing all that were oppressed of the devil; for GOD was with Him.

Acts 10:38.

And considering the chain of events on the day of Pentecost when all was there on one accord in one place. When the Holy Ghost, came, and they were all filled with the Spirit and begin to speak as the Holy Spirit gave them utterance. If my count of all nations present, it was sixteen nations under heaven. And these sixteen nations begin to hear the gospel of salvation from these 120 Galileans, that did not speak all these other languages, but the Holy Spirit spoke every language under heaven, through these Spirit filled, Galileans that those other nations might be saved.

Acts2:1-41.

Here is a verse of scripture that spoke to my understanding in these last days: Thus saith the LORD of hosts; In those days it shall come to pass, that ten men shall take hold out of all languages of the nations, even shall take hold of the skirt of him that is a Jew, saying, We will go with you for we have heard that GOD is with you.

Zechariah 8:23.

When the LORD GOD of the Hebrews told Moses, His faithful servant, I AM THE LORD, Moses understood that the LORD is an awesome GOD. The LORD is the Sovereign Ruler over the heaven of heavens, the Almighty GOD through out all the earth, and beneath the earth. The LORD is the Ultimate Authority over all thrones, all dominions, all principalities, all powers, whether visible, or invisible, the LORD is His name.

Colossians 1:15-17; Isaiah 42:8.

The Holy Spirit continue to say of the Holy Godhead (GOD the Father, GOD the Son, and GOD the Holy Spirit); there is none of the triune GOD named Jehovah.

Now therefore, what have I here, saith the LORD, that My people is taken away for nought? They that rule over them make them to howl, said the LORD; and My name continually every day is blasphemed.

Isaiah 52:5.

I AM THE LORD !

OF TRUTH AND RIGHTEOUSNESS

Our Blessed Savior and LORD JESUS CHRIST made this declaration of truth to His disciples pass, present, and future; He said: Henceforth I call you not servants; for the servant knoweth not what his LORD doeth: but I called you friends; for all things that I have heard of My Father I have made known unto you.

John 15:15.

And without controversy great is the mystery of godliness: GOD was manifest in the flesh, justified in the Spirit, seen of angels preached unto the Gentiles believed on in the world, received up into glory.

I Timothy 3:16.

And He hath on His vesture and on His thigh a name written, KING OF KINGS AND LORD OF LORDS.

Revelation 19:16.

I AM THE LORD!

Author Joseph L. Reaves Sr.

All Scripture is from the KJV.

NOTES: